Seven Years Old and Preparing for
BAPTISM

Seven Years Old and Preparing for
BAPTISM

Written and Illustrated by
GEORGE DURRANT

spring creek
BOOK COMPANY
Provo, Utah

© 2007 George Durrant
All Rights Reserved.

ISBN: 978-1-932898-74-3
e.1

Published by:
Spring Creek Book Company
P.O. Box 50355
Provo, Utah 84605-0355

www.springcreekbooks.com

Interior illustrations © George Durrant
Cover design © Spring Creek Book Company

Printed in the United States of America
10 9 8 7 6 5 4 3 2 1
Printed on acid-free paper

Dedication

To Hunter
and his grandma Glenna

Where it all happened:
1. Road that led one way to the school where I spilled my soup, and the other way to the roller coaster that scared me into using a bad word.
2. Road to Church where my teacher gave me an ice cream bar that I carried home to my mother to make up for being unkind to her.
3. My house where my mother loved and taught me.
4. The pasture where Herbie and I fought the Indians.
5. Herbie's house.
6. The place on the mountain where the airplane crashed.
7. Stick horses hoping to be unleashed so they could carry us off to an adventure.
8. Herbie and I in our happiest place, "The Old Apple Tree."
9. My dad's barn where I played basketball and got angry at my brother.
10. The pig that almost ate my brother's baseball mitt.
11. Allan's house where I read comic books.
12. The barn that burned down on the saddest day of my life.
13. Orval's house where we had his birthday party.
14. Our family's heroic dog named Brawn.
15. The grove of trees where we roasted our potatoes on sunny days.
16. Old creek bed where we went when we sluffed school, caught lizards, and made a faulty sun dial.
17. The cloud that I lied about.

Chapter 1

At Age Seven You Get Ready To Be Baptized.

When I was a little kid I never did have a birthday party. Hardly any kids in my town had birthday parties. One day I got a letter in the mail from my friend Orval's mother. The letter told me she was going to hold a

birthday party for Orval and I was invited to come. Orval lived across a big field and down the creek about a half mile. I was excited to go to the party, and as I was walking to Orval's house I wondered, "What will we do at Orval's birthday party?"

All I knew for sure was that Orval would have a big birthday cake and I would get a piece of that cake. It made me feel happy just thinking about it.

When I got to Orval's party there were six other boys there, all my same age. Each of them had brought a birthday present for Orval. I had forgotten to bring one. We played games at Orval's party. One game was to throw hoops over a pop bottle. I was good at that and I won a prize—a whistle. I blew it really hard and everybody put their hands over their ears. It was a really loud whistle. I decided to give it to Orval as a birthday gift. Orval said, "Thanks." He then blew the whistle and we all put our hands over our ears and laughed and laughed. Orval was happy and so was I.

Can you guess how old Orval was on the day of his party? I'll give you a clue. The next month Orval did something that was very important. He was baptized. Now can you guess how old Orval was on the day that I went to his birthday party? If you guessed eight, you are right.

I will never forget the day that I went to Orval's birthday party, because Orval was a year older that day. Every time someone has a birthday party they are always a year older. Even if they don't have a party on their birthday they are a year older. Being eight is very important because when you are eight you are old enough to be baptized.

You are not old enough to be baptized when you are five. You are not old enough when you are six, nor even seven. You have to be eight to be old enough to be baptized. Why does Heavenly Father want us to be eight before we get baptized?

This book tells us why.

Chapter 2

You Need to Be Ready Before You Get Baptized.

When I was one year old, I learned to walk.

When I was two, I learned to count to ten and to say my ABCs.

When I was three, I learned to dress myself and say my own prayers.

When I was four, I learned to write my own name but I was not quite ready to go to kindergarten.

Most children go to kindergarten at age five. I went to kindergarten when I was only four. I was frightened when my mother took me there. When my mother started to leave the classroom, I cried so hard my mother had to take me back home.

My father asked, "Why is George back home? He is supposed to be in kindergarten."

My mother replied, "I took him to kindergarten. When I told him I was going to go home, he said he wanted to go with me. I told him he had to stay. He started to cry and held on to my dress. He cried so hard the teacher told me that I should take him back home."

My father then asked her, "Will you take him back tomorrow?"

My mother replied, "No. I don't think he is old enough to be ready to go to kindergarten. He is not quite five years old. He is only four. I think we should wait a year until he is five. Then he will be ready to go to kindergarten."

The next year, when I was five, I went to kindergarten with a big smile on my face and did not even care when my mother left me there. By then I was ready for kindergarten because I was five.

When I was five, I was ready and I went to kindergarten and learned to play with clay and to color pictures with purple crayons.

When I was six, I went to the first grade. I learned to ride my two-wheel bike and to tie my own shoes, and I learned to read.

When I became seven, I went to the second grade. I kept learning things like how to add numbers and how to swim across the pool at the Saratoga Swimming Resort. I learned to shoot a basketball into the basket from a long ways away. But there were special things that I learned when I was seven. They were different than tying my shoe or reading a book or riding a bike or saying my ABCs. The things that I learned when I was seven were things I did not learn so much with my head or my body as I did with my heart. I learned things when I was seven that I was not ready to learn at age five or even at age

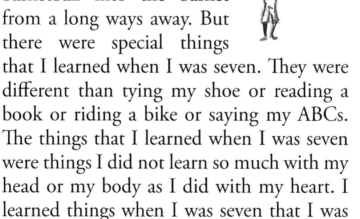

six. I learned things that I was not ready to learn until I was seven.

When I think of the things that I learned when I was seven, I understand why Heavenly Father told his Prophet Joseph Smith that the age for children to be baptized is eight years old. The special things I learned at age seven helped me to be ready to be baptized when I was eight. I hope that when you are eight that you will have a birthday party. But I hope even more, that when you are eight you will be baptized. If you are going to get baptized at age eight then what can you do when you are seven? You can do the things that will help you get ready to be baptized. This book will help you get ready to be baptized.

Let me tell you about the things that happened to me when I was seven years old. You will be amazed when you hear my story.

Chapter 3

Service

When You Learn to Help Others You Are More Prepared to Be Baptized.

When I was seven years old, I bought my school lunch. It cost three pennies, but I did not think that it was worth that much. One day school lunch was a bowl of tomato soup, the nastiest soup ever made. I got my soup and a little bottle of milk and headed for my table. But a kid pushed by and bumped me, and my bowl of soup fell off the tray and onto the hard cement. The bowl broke into hundreds of pieces and my smelly soup seemed to cover the whole lunch room floor.

My older brother Kent was in the sixth grade. He and his friends saw that I had spilled my soup and they started laughing and pointing at me. It seemed like every kid in that whole lunch room was laughing and pointing at me. I didn't know what to do. It was really sad for me. I was too old to cry, but that is what I wanted to do. Finally a lunch room lady came up with a mop and said, "You spilled it, you clean it up." As I was mopping, I knew that every kid in that place was looking at me and some of them were laughing. I felt worse than I had ever felt.

Finally a boy in my class named Bob came over to where I was mopping. He was not laughing. He said, "Sorry you spilled your soup. Let me have a turn helping to mop it up."

He took the mop and started to swish it back and forth. With him at my side I did not feel alone anymore. Everybody stopped looking at me, and nobody was laughing anymore. Pretty soon it was all cleaned up.

The lunch ladies gave me a new bowl of soup. I was not hungry, but I ate it anyway.

Back in class I kept looking over at Bob. I kept wishing I could help others the way that Bob had helped me.

That day, when I was seven years old, I learned something in my heart about helping others when they needed help like I did when everybody was laughing at me. Wanting to help others like Bob helped me made me be more prepared so that when I was eight I'd be ready to be baptized.

Chapter 4

Purity

When You Use Good Words You Are More Prepared to be Baptized.

I had a brother who was much older than me. When I was seven years old he was married and he was my bishop.

One day he and all of our family went to an amusement park called Lagoon. My brother Kent was ten and I was seven. Kent told me, "George, I just went on the roller coaster. It was the scariest thing I have ever done. You are too little, so don't go on it. It would scare you to death."

But I felt that if he could do it, I could do it too. I asked my older brother, the bishop, to take me on the roller coaster.

I got on the big car and held on tight. It slowly went up the hill making a click, click sound. I thought, "This is not scary." Then

we suddenly went over the top. It took my breath away as it fell at what seemed like ten thousand miles an hour. I was so afraid that I didn't know what to do.

I started to say over and over again a bad word that I had heard Nerk Conder say when I beat him at marbles. I could not stop saying that word.

Finally the roller coaster car slowed down and was not dropping any more. Then, as suddenly as it had done before, it went down again and out came the bad words.

I have never been as happy as I was when that thing finally stopped and I got off of it. My older brother took me by the hand and we went over and sat on a bench.

He looked at me and said, "How did you like that ride?"

"I liked it a lot," I replied.

"Do you want to ride it again?" he asked.

"No, I think I want to go on the Merry-Go-Round next," I answered.

He then asked, "What bad word did you say over and over again on the roller coaster?"

I said, "I don't know. I've never said that

word before, and I'll never say it again."

He smiled and told me that it would be a good idea for me to never use that word again.

I had been scared on that roller coaster. I felt bad that I had said that word. I decided that from then on I'd only use good words. I knew it would help me to only say good words if I stayed a mile away from the roller coaster.

That day when I was seven years old, I decided to try to not use bad words. so that when I was eight I'd be ready to be baptized.

Chapter 5

Honesty

When You Tell the Truth You Are More Prepared to be Baptized.

When I was seven years old I was in the second grade. Some days second graders only went to school until noon, and then they came home. Third graders and all those older than that had to go to school all day.

On one of the days when I only had to go to school until noon, I walked to school with my brother Kent. He and his two friends talked about doing something called "sluffing." Sluffing is when you leave home like you are going to school, but instead you go somewhere else and play all day. Then you go home and your mother thinks you have been at school.

Kent asked me if I wanted to sluff. It sounded fun and so I told him that I did.

It was a warm spring day and we headed up to the creek to play. We had a good time, but I felt like I should be in school.

We caught about seven lizards under an old car door. We threw rocks in the creek. It was fun, but I still felt like I should be in school.

Finally my brother said, "I need to make

a sundial so we can see what time it is. If it is 12 o'clock then George needs to go home or our mother will wonder where he is."

He stuck a stick in the ground and looked at its shadow. After much study he and his friends agreed that it was noon, the time that I should go on home.

When I got to the front porch of our house my mother came out the door and asked, "Why are you home an hour early?"

I did not know what to say. I looked down and then I looked up at the sky. I saw

one little white cloud in the sky. I told my mother, "See that cloud? My teacher saw it too and she said that it might rain and so we should all go home."

My mother came close to me and said, "George, look at me. Your teacher did not say that. You are not telling the truth. Where have you been?"

At the risk of being in trouble with my brother, I told her that we had all sluffed. I could tell that she was really sad. She told me, "George, don't you ever lie to me again."

I decided then and there that I would

never sluff again. And then I would never have to lie to my mother again. I decided to always tell the truth. That day, when I was seven, I was a bit more prepared to be baptized.

Chapter 6

Responsibility

When You Become Responsible You Are More Prepared to be Baptized.

When I was seven years old I got into the biggest trouble I have ever been in. My older brother Kent, our friend Allen, and I liked to make a bonfire out under the trees near

my house. Then we would throw a potato in the fire. In a few minutes we would get a long stick and push the potato out of the fire. It would be burned black.

We would let it cool for a few minutes and then we would peel the black skin off the potato. Then we would eat the cooked potato. Potatoes cooked that way are really good to eat.

One day we looked out of the window and it was raining. We knew we could not make the bonfire in the rain, and so we couldn't cook the potatoes.

But we tried anyway. We walked to the grove of trees and the wood was too wet to build the fire. That made us sad because we wanted to have cooked potatoes.

Allen said, "We can go over to my grandfather's barn and build a fire in there. It will be nice and dry inside the barn."

Kent agreed, "That is a good idea." We all picked up our potatoes and ran over to the barn.

We got some wood from the wood shed and took it into the barn. Pretty soon we had a blazing fire inside the barn. Soon our potatoes were cooked. We peeled them and ate them. They seemed more delicious than any potatoes we had ever cooked before.

We put out the fire, then Kent and I went home.

An hour later the fire engine went by our house. I have never heard the fire siren sound so loud. My fifteen-year-old brother John came running into the house and shouted, "Allen's barn is on fire!"

My father asked Kent, "Have you kids been up there playing with matches?"

I crawled behind our big stove where I always went to hide. My mother looked out the window and said, "Oh no! The whole barn is on fire." I tried to disappear into the stove.

Pretty soon Allen's barn and all their family's other sheds were all burned down.

I was sure that the firemen and the police would find out that I had done it. I would be sent to jail. I was the most frightened and sad I had ever been. I kept wishing that we had not gone to the barn and made that fire.

Soon everyone found out what had happened. My father said that it was Kent's fault. He said, "Kent is ten years old. He is old enough to be responsible." He added, "George is only seven. He is not old enough to know what he is doing."

That made me feel a little better, but it sure did make Kent feel bad. The next few days I kept thinking about how we had burned down the barn, wishing that we had never done it.

I knew that what my father said was not quite right. My father said that I was seven and did not know that we should not build a fire in a barn. The truth was that I did know better. I should have said, "Let's not

build a fire in a barn. Building a fire in a barn could send a spark that could catch the barn on fire." I knew I should have said that, but I wanted a cooked potato, so I did not say anything.

Kent probably knew that we should not build a fire in the barn. So did our friend Allen. All I could think about was that I was responsible. I might not have been responsible at age five or age six, but I was seven and I knew it was not right to build a fire in a barn. I was old enough to be responsible.

A month later there was a grass fire over by the creek. I went over there to watch the firemen put out the fire. One of the firemen said to another, "It looks like those darn Durrant kids have been over here playing with matches again."

When he said that and I heard what he said. I felt really bad. I never wanted to be called a "darned Durrant kid" again—I wanted to be called a good Durrant kid. I wanted to be a Durrant kid who did good things. I did not want to be a kid who did things that were dumb . . . things like building a fire inside a barn.

I know we should not have done such a bad thing. Doing that bad thing taught me a lesson. I knew more than I had ever known before that I was old enough to know what was right and what was wrong. Knowing that, when I was seven years old, made it so that I was about ready to be baptized.

Chapter 6

Repentance

When You Try to Make Others Happy, You Are More Prepared to be Baptized.

When I was seven I used to like to play in my father's barn. My older brothers put a basketball hoop up in our barn. I would go out there and shoot the basketball at the hoop. I did that so often that I got so I could make a basket nearly every time that I shot the ball.

I usually played basketball in the barn all by myself. Then one day my older brother Kent came and said he would play me a game to see who could shoot the best. He made five shots in a row and I made six. I had won the game. He said that I had only made four and that he had won the game. He then walked out of the barn and headed for the house. I was crying because I knew that I had won and he had lost. I was really angry, and I told him I had won. He laughed and said I was wrong, and that he had won.

He had just bought a new baseball mitt with money he had earned. He loved his new mitt. I saw that he had left his mitt in the barn. So I picked it up and threw it out the window into the pig pen.

Later he remembered that he had left his mitt in the barn and so he went out to get it. In a little while, he came back in and asked me where I had put the mitt. I told him I

had not put his mitt anywhere. I told him that it might be out in the pig pen.

He ran out to the pig pen. Pretty soon he came back to the house. He was really mad and very sad. The pig had thought that the mitt was food and had torn the mitt inside out. The mitt was all covered with dirt and mud and other stuff.

My brother held the mitt up between his finger and his thumb and said, "Look

what you have done! My mitt is ruined. You ruined it by throwing it into the pig pen."

I was sad that I had done that. He asked me if doing such a bad thing made me happy.

I said that it did make me happy, but inside I was as sad as he was. I knew how much he loved his mitt. I kept wishing I had not done what I had done. I did not say that to him. Sometimes it is hard to tell the truth about how you feel when you have done a bad thing.

Later I gathered all of the money I had been saving to buy a new ball, and I gave him the money. I did not say I was sorry. It was always really hard to say that I was sorry. But he could tell that I was sorry and so we were friends again. The next day he bought a new mitt and I was happy for him.

That day, when I was seven, I knew that doing bad things made me sad inside. Those kinds of feelings made me want to do whatever I could do to make people who I made sad feel happy again. Those kinds of feelings that I had when I was seven years old made it so I was about ready to be baptized.

Chapter 7

Generosity

When You Are Not Selfish You Are More Prepared to be Baptized.

When I was seven years old, we had a dog named Brawn. He was a big German Shepard dog. He was yellow like gold. He lived with our family for ten years before I was born and he was still living there when I was seven.

Mother told me once, a few years before, that Brawn had saved Kent's life. She said that when Kent was a little boy he ran away from home and went down a busy street. Brawn followed him and kept pushing him off to the side of the street so that the passing cars would not hit him.

A neighbor man saw all of this and told my parents about what Brawn had done. Brawn was a hero.

Brawn would walk to school with me. I loved Brawn more than I had ever loved anything before. I told mother that Brawn was my dog. She replied, "No, he is not your dog. He is everybody in the family's dog."

I told Kent that Brawn was my dog and he replied, "He is my dog. He saved my life."

I answered, "He goes to school with me. After school he helps me cross the railroad tracks safely. He likes me best. He is my dog."

Kent replied, "You think that you own everything. You are the most selfish little kid in the whole world. You won't let anybody play with any of your stuff. You are selfish. Brawn does not like selfish people. So he is my dog, not yours."

Kent had a way of making me real angry. The reason I would not let others play with my stuff is because it was my stuff, not theirs. I did not want others to play with my stuff.

Brawn was getting old. He got hit by a truck and that made him lame. Then he ate some poison that a farmer put out to protect his sheep from dogs. Brawn would just lay there, so I would go out and pet him and tell him how much I loved him. I told him that I knew he would get better.

My father told us all at dinner that Brawn was in pain and that he should be put down. My uncle came and Dad told him to take Brawn to a lonely place and shoot him to put him out of his misery. He told him to take a shovel and bury Brawn by a big tree.

I started to cry and told everybody, "No. You can't shoot Brawn. He is my dog. I will take care of him. You can't shoot him."

My mother said, "Brawn is in pain. He can hardly breathe and he whines and cries."

I ran out of the house and as I did I told everyone there, "I hate you all. You don't love Brawn the way that I do."

I stayed out in the trees until it was dark. I cried my eyes out because I knew I would never see Brawn again. Finally I came back to the house.

That night when our family was all together, we all looked at a picture of Brawn.

Each one of us told how much we loved our faithful dog Brawn. My older brother Kent started to talk about Brawn and then he could not talk because he was so sad.

When I saw Kent so sad, something inside of me told me that Kent loved Brawn as much as I did. Then I knew that Brawn was not my dog. He was our family's dog. He belonged to all of us.

I knew that I had been a coward by

running away when I could have told Brawn goodbye. I knew that I had been selfish. I decided I would try not being so selfish. I decided I would share things that I owned so that others could be happy. Having those kinds of feelings when I was seven years old made it so I was more ready to be baptized than I had ever been before.

Chapter.8

Obedience

When You Honor Your Parents You Are More Prepared to be Baptized.

When I was seven we used to have Primary on Tuesday afternoon. Now we have it on Sunday morning.

I loved Primary. I would go every week. I was given an award because I never did miss Primary for two years.

One day I did not want to go to Primary. My mother told me that I must go. I told her I did not want to go.

She told me that if I did not go to Primary, I had to come in the house and that I could not play with the other kids. I told her that I wanted to play.

She came out and told me I had to come in the house. I could tell that I had no choice, so I went into the house.

I said to my mother, "You never let me do what I want to do. You always tell me what to do."

She told me that she just wanted me to do good things.

I did not like being inside, so I decided to go to Primary. When I walked out the door to go, she said, "George, thanks for being a good boy." Then she said, "I love you."

I didn't even look back and I did not tell her that I loved her.

It was a hot day and we were really happy when our Primary teacher said, "You have been such good boys that I have brought you some ice cream bars. You will have to eat them fast or they will melt."

I felt happy. Going to Primary always made me happy once I got there. I felt bad that I had been kind of mean to my mother. Then I had an idea. I decided I would take the ice cream bar home to mother to show her that I loved her.

I put the ice cream bar in my pocket and ran home. By the time I got there I could feel something running down my leg.

When I saw my mother I shouted, "I have got something for you." I reached in

my pocket to give her the ice cream bar. All I could feel was some sticky, runny stuff. I pulled my pocket inside out. All that was there was the stick. I showed it to Mother and she laughed. She said, "You should have eaten it and not brought it home for me."

She got me some clean pants to change into, and then she held me on her lap in the big rocking chair. She held me close and told me how much it meant to her to have me try to bring the ice cream bar home to her. Then she said, "You don't have to bring me stuff to show me you love me. All you have to do to show me that you love me is try to be a good boy and to tell me that you love me."

I softly said, "I do love you."

She held me even tighter.

That day when I was seven I knew how happy it made me when I felt close to my parents and honored them. That day when I was seven I was a bit more prepared to be baptized.

Chapter 9

Prayerful

When You Know Why We Pray You Are More Prepared To be Baptized.

One night my father was gone to his job and my older brothers were also gone. I was home alone with my mother. I could tell that something was wrong. I could see tears in my mother's eyes.

She told me that she had to go lie down on her bed. I could hear her crying.

After what seemed like a long time my older brother Stewart and his wife, Leola, came to visit.

I told them mother was in bed and that she was crying. My brother went in to see what was wrong. Pretty soon he came out and said, "Mother is in great pain. I must go get a neighbor man. Then we will give Mother a Priesthood blessing."

Pretty soon he came back with the other man. I stood in the doorway and they laid their hands on Mother's head. They asked Heavenly Father to bless her.

I could only hear part of the prayer. I felt something that I had never felt before.

The next morning at breakfast my mother told me, "I was in such pain. I did not know what I would do. But when Stewart laid his hands on my head and gave me a blessing, the pain left. And all night long I was able to sleep. This morning I feel all better."

She then told me, "Your older brother has the power of the Priesthood. The power of the priesthood is the power of God. I hope you will grow up and have the power of the Priesthood. You are such a good boy that you will be able to help others the way that Stewart helped me."

My older brother Stewart could play sports, and he was handsome and big. He was good to me and I loved him. I wanted to be able to be good at sports. I wanted to look like him. Most of all I wanted to be like him. I wanted to have the power of the Priesthood so that if my mother ever got sick I would be able to give her a blessing like he did and make her all better.

I was so glad to know that Heavenly Father made it so we can pray and he will listen and help us. That day, when I was seven years old, I was a bit more prepared to be baptized.

Chapter 10

Loyalty

When You Learn to Be a Good Friend You Are More Prepared to Be Baptized.

When I was seven years old, on the first day of summer vacation I made myself a new stick horse. The one I had ridden the last summer was named Trigger. Trigger was getting old. He was not as fast as he had been last summer.

Early in the morning I went to the little stream where the willows grew along the bank. I cut off a long green willow with my pocket knife. I knew that this was going to be the best horse that ever had been in our town.

Then I went home and carved him a wooden head out of a thin piece of cardboard. I nailed the head onto the willow. I called my new horse Silver.

Then I went up to my best friend Herbie's house. I helped him make his horse. He named his horse Scout.

That first week of summer, we rode those horses on Monday, Tuesday, Wednesday, Thursday and Friday. We pretended there were a whole bunch of Indians up past our chicken coop. We pretended there were some bank robbers up by Allen's ponds. We were really good at pretending.

During those first five days of summer, we had ten battles with those Indians. They finally gave up and ran off in a cloud of dust headed for Idaho.

Then we took on the robbers. They were no match for Herbie and me and our stick horses, which were the fastest two horses in the town.

Then one day a boy named Alan came to live with his grandfather and grandmother. Alan lived in Salt Lake City. He would come down and stay with his grandparents in the summer.

Alan did not like stick horses or other fun stuff. He just liked to sit in the log shed and read comic books. He brought more than a hundred of them with him so he would have stuff to do all summer. He invited me up to read some of them. They did not make sense to me. I just felt that stories of going to other planets and men flying around like birds were not true, and I did not want to read any false stuff. I wanted to stick to things like the Lone Ranger and other true stories.

I started to be Alan's friend. He knew a lot about big cities and street cars and other things that I did not know much about.

When Herbie would come to see me, I'd tell him that I was going up to see Alan. I could tell that Herbie wanted to go with me,

but I didn't know if Alan would like that. I told Herbie I'd see him later. I took off and just left him standing there. Since I turned seven I did not like doing stuff like making others sad. As I walked away, I almost turned back to get Herbie, but I did not.

I read comic books with Alan for two hours. Then something inside of me made me start thinking about how much fun I always had when I played with Herbie.

I told Alan I had to go home. He just kept reading his comic book like he didn't care if I left.

I went home. But I just went there long

enough to get on my stick horse to ride up to see Herbie. Herbie was sitting on his porch all alone. When he saw me riding up on Silver, he got a big smile on his face. I told him to get his horse because the Indians had come back. And we needed to save the pioneers from an attack.

We rode off in a cloud of dust. Our horses Silver and Scout ran faster that day than they had ever run before. It was so good to be back with my friend Herbie.

That day when I was seven I was so happy to know that I was a good friend to Herbie. I liked to be a good friend who wanted my friends to be as happy as I was. When I learned to be a good friend, I was getting more ready to be baptized.

Chapter 11

Compassion

When You Try to Help Others You Are More Prepared to be Baptized.

One Friday night after dinner, it came on the news that an airplane had crashed on the mountain. It said that the pilot was killed and that he had a nice wife and a son just my age.

That night when we gathered for our family prayer my mother said, "Dear Heavenly Father, please bless the wife and the little son of the man who was killed in the airplane crash."

That night in my bedroom, I could not go to sleep, I just kept thinking of that boy. I was glad that my dad was not on that airplane.

I felt really bad for that boy whose dad had been the pilot of the plane. I wished I could call him on the phone or write him a letter and tell him how sad I felt for him.

As I laid there in bed, I tried to think of all the fun Herbie and I would have tomorrow. I also kept thinking of the boy. He would never be able to go fishing with his dad again. I'd never felt bad like that when I was five years old or even when I was six. Now that I was seven, I was almost starting to cry when I fell asleep.

The next morning Herbie and I went over to the apple tree. We took a salt shaker and picked some little green apples to eat. We were going to have fun that day.

Herbie said, "Let's get going. My horse is ready for a good gallop." I just sat there on the ditch bank with my bare feet dangling in the swiftly moving water.

I was thinking about that airplane and the boy whose dad was gone. I had an idea

to make that boy a stick horse. I would have done it but I did not know what the boy's name was or even where he lived.

So I got on old Silver and Herbie and I rode off toward the canal to make sure the Indians had not returned. I shouted, "Hi ho Silver." Herbie shouted, "Get um up, Scout."

That afternoon I went to the ditch bank and cut a lone straight willow. I went home and drew a horse head on cardboard. I showed my mother what I had done and told her that I wanted to make a stick horse for that boy.

"What boy?" she asked.

"The boy whose dad died."

She told me that I was a good boy. She then said, "I think if you asked Heavenly Father to bless and help him that that would be even better than a stick horse." So that is what I did.

My being seven years old, instead of being five or six, helped me to understand more than I ever could before about how other people being sad made me sad. Those kinds of feelings helped me be more prepared to be baptized.

My Wish and Prayer for You

When I was seven years old, Heavenly Father taught me the things that I needed to know to be baptized. In Primary I learned many things about Heavenly Father and Jesus. I learned more about prayer, and paying tithing, and going to church and living the Word of Wisdom. My parents taught me these same things.

However, when I was seven years old, it was the things that I learned in real life—the things I have told you in this book—that were among the most important things that helped me be prepared to be baptized.

On October 20th 1939, I was no longer seven years old. On that day, I had a birthday. I became eight years old. I did not have a birthday party like Orval did, but I was eight years old. Two weeks later I was prepared and I was ready to be baptized. On November 1st 1939, I was baptized. That made me very happy.

I know that when you become eight years old, you will be prepared and that you will be baptized. I know that you will be as happy as I was.